Set design by Si Joong Yoon   Photo by Beth Lincks

Benim Foster and Alexandra Geis in a scene from
the New York production of *Last Train to Nibroc*.

LAST TRAIN TO NIBROC

BY
ARLENE HUTTON

DRAMATISTS
PLAY SERVICE
INC.

Last Train to Nibroc
Copyright © 2000, Arlene Hutton

All Rights Reserved

CAUTION: Professionals and amateurs are hereby warned that performance of LAST TRAIN TO NIBROC is subject to payment of a royalty. It is fully protected under the copyright laws of the United States of America, and of all countries covered by the International Copyright Union (including the Dominion of Canada and the rest of the British Commonwealth), and of all countries covered by the Pan-American Copyright Convention, the Universal Copyright Convention, the Berne Convention, and of all countries with which the United States has reciprocal copyright relations. All rights, including without limitation professional/amateur stage rights, motion picture, recitation, lecturing, public reading, radio broadcasting, television, video or sound recording, all other forms of mechanical, electronic and digital reproduction, transmission and distribution, such as CD, DVD, the Internet, private and file-sharing networks, information storage and retrieval systems, photocopying, and the rights of translation into foreign languages are strictly reserved. Particular emphasis is placed upon the matter of readings, permission for which must be secured from the Author's agent in writing.

The English language stock and amateur stage performance rights in the United States, its territories, possessions and Canada for LAST TRAIN TO NIBROC are controlled exclusively by DRAMATISTS PLAY SERVICE, INC., 440 Park Avenue South, New York, NY 10016. No professional or nonprofessional performance of the Play may be given without obtaining in advance the written permission of DRAMATISTS PLAY SERVICE, INC., and paying the requisite fee.

Inquiries concerning all other rights should be addressed to Beacon Artists Agency, 120 East 56th Street, Suite 540, New York, NY 10022. Attn: Patricia McLaughlin.

SPECIAL NOTE

Anyone receiving permission to produce LAST TRAIN TO NIBROC is required to give credit to the Author as sole and exclusive Author of the Play on the title page of all programs distributed in connection with performances of the Play and in all instances in which the title of the Play appears for purposes of advertising, publicizing or otherwise exploiting the Play and/or a production thereof. The name of the Author must appear on a separate line, in which no other name appears, immediately beneath the title and in size of type equal to 50% of the size of the largest, most prominent letter used for the title of the Play. No person, firm or entity may receive credit larger or more prominent than that accorded the Author. The following acknowledgment must appear on the title page in all programs distributed in connection with performances of the Play:

> LAST TRAIN TO NIBROC was originally workshopped with the help of a development grant from Loyola Marymount University. It was first showcased at the New York International Fringe Festival, a presentation of The Present Company, and further workshopped at New Dramatists, premiering at the 78th Street Theatre Lab in a co-production with The Journey Company.
>
> The play was subsequently produced Off-Broadway by Leonard Soloway, Chase Mishkin, and Steven M. Levy.

*For my parents,
Arlie and Mary Elizabeth Lincks,
with love and thanks*

AUTHOR'S NOTE

The idea for the first scene of *Last Train to Nibroc* came to me while reading a biography of S. J. Perelman, who was a brother-in-law to the author Nathanael West. West died in a car accident in December 1940, and his body was shipped east by train. Also on the same train was Sheila Graham, for her companion F. Scott Fitzgerald had also passed away, and it is very likely that she was accompanying his body across the country to Maryland.

I put two young people from Kentucky on that train, basing them very loosely on my parents, who in real life had been falling in love at just about that time. *Last Train to Nibroc* is a patchwork quilt of family lore and stories I heard as a child, all stitched together to tell the fictional tale of May and Raleigh. When I wrote the one-act version, which is the first scene of the full-length, I had no idea how the details about Raleigh and May would pay off later. Indeed, May was originally called "Mary." An early typo amended it to "May," and I liked that better, not realizing that it would be important in Scene Three. When setting up Raleigh's epilepsy in the first scene, I also had no idea, until I read it on my computer screen, that Raleigh would become ill at the end of Scene Two, or that May would misunderstand his sickness in the way she does. Moments like these were as much a surprise to me when I wrote them as they are for the audience seeing the play.

It has been extremely rewarding to see the audience response to this little play. The senior citizens are delighted to revisit their past, of course, but I have especially enjoyed the enthusiasm of teens and young adults who gain insight into the lives of their parents or grandparents, discovering that the "good old days" were not so simple and that stories of love and forgiveness are universal to all ages.

Arlene Hutton
New York City
June 11, 1999

LAST TRAIN TO NIBROC was produced by Leonard Soloway, Chase Mishkin, and Steven M. Levy at the Douglas Fairbanks Theatre in New York City on November 21, 1999. It was directed by Michael Montel; the set design was by Si Joong Yoon; the lighting design was by Christopher Gorzelnik; the sound design was by Peter J. Fitzgerald; the costume design was by Shelley Norton; and the stage manager was Tamara K. Heeschen. The cast was as follows:

RALEIGH .... Benim Foster
MAY .... Alexandra Geis

LAST TRAIN TO NIBROC received its premiere at the 78th Street Theatre Lab in New York City on February 11, 1999. It was co-produced by the 78th Street Theatre Lab (Eric Nightengale, Artistic Director) and The Journey Company (Beth Lincks, Producing Artistic Director). It was directed by Michael Montel; the lighting design was by Christopher Gorzelnik; the costume design was by Shelley Norton; and the stage manager was Julie Kessler. The cast was as follows:

RALEIGH .... Benim Foster
MAY .... Alexandra Geis

LAST TRAIN TO NIBROC was presented at the Assembly Rooms for the Edinburgh Festival Fringe 1999 and at the Piccolo Spoleto Theatre Festival 2000. It was produced by The Journey Company and the 78th Street Theatre Lab. It was directed by Michael Montel; the lighting design was by Eric Nightengale; the costume design was by Shelley Norton; and the stage manager was James Thaggard. The cast was as follows:

RALEIGH .... Benim Foster
MAY .... Alexandra Geis

LAST TRAIN TO NIBROC was originally workshopped at The Players through a development grant from Loyola Marymount, with Benim Foster and Alexandra Geis, under the direction of Judith Royer. A showcase production with Benim Foster and Alexandra Geis, under the direction of Michael Montel, was presented at the Henry Street Settlement for the New York International Fringe Festival 1998, a presentation of The Present Company.

CHARACTERS

MAY — Twenty-one or twenty-two. From a small town in Kentucky. She is sincere and honest in her beliefs.

RALEIGH — About the same age. From a nearby town. Just a good guy, slow to anger and quick to chuckle.

Note: For alternative casting purposes, the two actors should be of the same ethnicity.

PLACE

A park bench could be used for all three scenes with covers placed on it for Scenes One and Three, creating a train seat and a porch settee or swing.

TIME

SCENE ONE
December 28, 1940
A train, somewhere west of Chicago

SCENE TWO
Summer 1942
A park bench near a woods.

SCENE THREE
Spring 1943
May's front porch.

The play is to be performed without intermission. If that is not possible, the interval break should occur between Scene One and Scene Two.

Pronunciation note: "Nibroc" rhymes with "rib rock," with the accent on the first syllable.

LAST TRAIN TO NIBROC

SCENE ONE

December 28th, 1940. Two train seats on a train bound from California to Chicago. May, twenty-one or twenty-two, is seated by the window, reading a book. Raleigh, close in age, is standing next to her, in the aisle. He wears a flyer's uniform. They both have slight Kentucky accents. He looks at her, as though expecting her to say something. She is very shy with strangers.

RALEIGH. Mind if I ... *(May keeps reading her book.)* Mind if I set a spell? *(Raleigh gestures to the empty seat beside her.)*
MAY. *(After a beat.)* Don't make no nevermind to me. *(May keeps reading her book. A pause.)*
RALEIGH. This train —
MAY. Yes?
RALEIGH. This train's very —
MAY. Yes, it's —
RALEIGH. Full. Crowded.
MAY. Yes.
RALEIGH. *(Smiling at her.)* I was lucky to get a seat.
MAY. Yes. *(Looking around.)* But —
RALEIGH. Do you mind me sitting here?
MAY. I don't know you.
RALEIGH. I was standing all night.
MAY. Standing?
RALEIGH. Until the train stopped at this station.
MAY. Yes, it was full —
RALEIGH. It was packed leaving California. I got on in Los Angelees. *(Pause.)* What ya reading?
MAY. Pardon?

RALEIGH. Your book.
MAY. Oh. *(May looks at the cover of the book.)* It's *Magnificent Obsession*.
RALEIGH. *(Gently teasing.)* Sounds pretty racy.
MAY. *(Taking him seriously.)* No. Not at all.
RALEIGH. A romance.
MAY. It's more religious …
RALEIGH. *(Still teasing.)* There's no romance in it?
MAY. It's not about that.
RALEIGH. There's not a girl and a guy?
MAY. Well, there is, but —
RALEIGH. It must be a love story.
MAY. It's not. I don't read —
RALEIGH. It's a love story. Has to be.
MAY. *(Flustered.)* Why?
RALEIGH. With a title like that. *Magnificent Obsession*.
MAY. That's not what the title is about.
RALEIGH. Not what?
MAY. Not about.
RALEIGH. Not about what?
MAY. Romance. A love story. What you — It's not about — *(She pauses.)*
RALEIGH. *(Simply.)* What is it about? Your book. What's it about?
MAY. This man — *(She stops.)*
RALEIGH. Do they kiss?
MAY. What?
RALEIGH. In the book?
MAY. *(Simply.)* I haven't finished it yet.
RALEIGH. Oh.
MAY. But it's religious.
RALEIGH. Uh-huh.
MAY. It is. It's from the church library. The library at church. It's religious. *(May goes back to her book. A pause.)*
RALEIGH. Are you?
MAY. What?
RALEIGH. Religious?
MAY. Well, yes.

RALEIGH. *(Pause.)* It's about a doctor. *(Pause.)* Your book.
MAY. You've read it!
RALEIGH. A couple years ago. I read everything.
MAY. Don't tell me the ending.
RALEIGH. It's a romance.
MAY. No, it's —
RALEIGH. Religious?
MAY. Well, inspirational. *(A pause.)*
RALEIGH. You like to read?
MAY. Well, yes.
RALEIGH. I like to write.
MAY. *(Interested.)* Really? You're a writer?
RALEIGH. Gonna be. *(Pause.)* There's writers on this train.
MAY. How do you know?
RALEIGH. Porter over yonder told me. He let me sit in the men's room for a while.
MAY. I thought you didn't have a seat.
RALEIGH. That's good.
MAY. What is?
RALEIGH. That's funny.
MAY. It's not funny that you had to sit in the —
RALEIGH. I thought it was lucky. Like having a private room.
MAY. A private room with running water.
RALEIGH. With hot and cold running water.
MAY. *(Laughs.)* You're funny.
RALEIGH. So're you. *(They smile at each other. A pause. May picks up her book again.)* The porter told me there's writers on the train.
MAY. Riders? People riding the train?
RALEIGH. Writers. Authors.
MAY. Well, there's lots of people on the train.
RALEIGH. Guess who's riding this train with us.
MAY. I don't like to guess.
RALEIGH. No, just guess. You can't.
MAY. I know I can't guess, so I won't even try.
RALEIGH. Two of them.
MAY. Writers or riders?
RALEIGH. Authors. Famous ones.
MAY. Who?

RALEIGH. Guess!
MAY. I don't — *(May reads from the spine of her book.)* Lloyd C. Douglas?
RALEIGH. Nope.
MAY. William Shakespeare?
RALEIGH. You're not even trying.
MAY. I don't care.
RALEIGH. Very famous writers.
MAY. Who, then?
RALEIGH. Nathanael West!
MAY. Who's that?
RALEIGH. You don't know who Nathanael West is?
MAY. No.
RALEIGH. He's a great novelist. *The Day of the Locust. Miss Lonelyhearts.*
MAY. I don't read books like that.
RALEIGH. Books like what?
MAY. Lonely heart books. Romances.
RALEIGH. They're not — What do you read? Besides … *(Raleigh indicates her book.)*
MAY. Inspirational stories.
RALEIGH. F. Scott Fitzgerald.
MAY. No.
RALEIGH. He inspired me.
MAY. That's not what I meant.
RALEIGH. He's on this train, too.
MAY. Is not.
RALEIGH. Is so. F. Scott Fitzgerald is riding on this train. Going to New York City.
MAY. You're making it up.
RALEIGH. Do you even know who he is?
MAY. Of course.
RALEIGH. Have you read his books?
MAY. No.
RALEIGH. Well, he's on this train. F. Scott Fitzgerald.
MAY. But he's dead, silly. He died. He died a few days ago. I read about it in the newspaper. *(A slight pause.)*
RALEIGH. He's on the train.

MAY. He's dead.
RALEIGH. He's in the baggage car. *(A pause.)*
MAY. You're crazy.
RALEIGH. His coffin.
MAY. Pardon?
RALEIGH. His coffin is riding in the baggage car. F. Scott Fitzgerald is on this train. He's riding the same train we are.
MAY. Oh. *(Pause.)* How do you know?
RALEIGH. Porter told me.
MAY. Oh.
RALEIGH. With Nathanael West.
MAY. He's with him?
RALEIGH. His coffin, too. We're riding with two of the greatest authors of the century. We're all on this train together.
MAY. That's morbid.
RALEIGH. It's funny, what puts people on trains together.
MAY. Mmmm. *(May looks out the window.)* Where are we?
RALEIGH. Don't know. *(Raleigh tries to look out her window.)* Can't tell. But the sun's about to come up.
MAY. It's black as pitch.
RALEIGH. Little light over yonder. See? Just a glimpse of a sunrise. *(He leans over her even more to see out.)*
MAY. You can't have this seat.
RALEIGH. *(Surprised.)* I don't want it.
MAY. Well, you can't have it!
RALEIGH. I never said —
MAY. You just want the window seat so you can sleep. Lean your head against the window.
RALEIGH. No, it's yours.
MAY. You're right. It's mine. And I'm not giving it up.
RALEIGH. Look, miss.
MAY. *(Starting to cry.)* I came all the way out here sitting on the aisle seat. People bumping me and I never got to sleep at all and I couldn't look out the window most of the time and there were small children running around. I like children —
RALEIGH. — of course you do —
MAY. — but not when they're running up and down the aisles a' screaming. And bumping my arm so I couldn't sleep for the life of

me, not even doze, and there was this man —
RALEIGH. — a man?
MAY. — for hours, just hours, in the window seat here, and I couldn't find another seat, and I had to sit up straight and he —
RALEIGH. — what?
MAY. *(Really crying now.)* — he smelled. He just smelled bad. And the train and the smell made me sick and I had to — well, I almost had to, well, be sick.
RALEIGH. Oh, that's too bad.
MAY. But I wasn't. And so I'm not giving up this seat to anyone, not my window seat, not to anyone, especially not to a soldier! *(A pause.)*
RALEIGH. Would you like my handkerchief?
MAY. I have my own, thank you very much.
RALEIGH. May I get it for you? Your handkerchief.
MAY. *(Sobbing.)* It's in my suitcase. *(She looks up towards the overhead shelf.)*
RALEIGH. Here's mine, then. Take it. You need a handkerchief.
MAY. I'm just so tired. I don't know what to do.
RALEIGH. *(At a loss.)* Uh-huh.
MAY. It's been so awful.
RALEIGH. It will get better.
MAY. I don't see how. *(Pause.)* I have to go home.
RALEIGH. Well, that's good, isn't it?
MAY. I don't know how I can face them. My family.
RALEIGH. Please don't mind my asking this.
MAY. You're being very nice. And you don't even know me.
RALEIGH. You're afraid to go home to your family.
MAY. Not afraid. Ashamed.
RALEIGH. Is there? ... Are you? ... You felt ill.
MAY. No.
RALEIGH. On the trip out. You said ...
MAY. You think I'm ... delicate?
RALEIGH. You said that you —
MAY. Oh, no. I'd never. How can you think that of me?
RALEIGH. I don't.
MAY. They'll think that.
RALEIGH. Your family.

MAY. They'll think that we … that I. *(May starts to sob again.)*
RALEIGH. But you're not.
MAY. Of course not!
RALEIGH. Well, that's good then.
MAY. We were engaged.
RALEIGH. A soldier.
MAY. Well, he's training. To fly. Yes.
RALEIGH. You went out to see him. Before he went to England.
MAY. Yes. For Christmas.
RALEIGH. That was a nice thing for you to do.
MAY. No. He was different. He's changed. *(A pause.)*
RALEIGH. And now you're going home.
MAY. Yes.
RALEIGH. Home, where? Where's home?
MAY. Kentucky. Corbin. Corbin, Kentucky.
RALEIGH. No.
MAY. Yes. Corbin.
RALEIGH. I'm from Woodbine, Kentucky.
MAY. You're not.
RALEIGH. Yes, I am.
MAY. Well, how about that.
RALEIGH. How about that. Just a few miles apart.
MAY. So you're going to Woodbine?
RALEIGH. No, I'm just from there. I'm going to New York City.
MAY. You're not changing trains?
RALEIGH. No, I was. In the beginning. Almost. But I want to go to New York City.
MAY. You out of the service?
RALEIGH. Um, well, yeah.
MAY. Aren't you itching to go? Go overseas?
RALEIGH. I was.
MAY. Most people volunteering. Going into the service. I don't know anybody leaving the service.
RALEIGH. Medical. *(A pause.)*
MAY. I'm sorry. *(An awkward pause.)*
RALEIGH. It was hard to leave my buddies.
MAY. I would imagine it was. But don't you want to see your family?

RALEIGH. They'll be ashamed I'm not off flying like I said I was gonna do.
MAY. They'd be glad to see you.
RALEIGH. They'll think I gave up.
MAY. No. They'll be glad you didn't go fight. They'll be real glad to see you.
RALEIGH. Later. After I've been in New York City for a while.
MAY. Don't you miss Kentucky? I missed Corbin. When I was in California.
RALEIGH. Corbin's a nice town. The Nibroc festival.
MAY. I've never been.
RALEIGH. You've never been to the Nibroc festival?
MAY. No.
RALEIGH. And you grew up in Corbin.
MAY. Yes.
RALEIGH. Lived in Corbin all your life?
MAY. Yes.
RALEIGH. And you've never been to the Nibroc festival?
MAY. No. Have you?
RALEIGH. Sure.
MAY. I haven't.
RALEIGH. Why not?
MAY. I always went to the tent meeting. It's the same time of year. I went to the tent meetings at the campgrounds. To hear all the preachers.
RALEIGH. You "saved"?
MAY. Of course. You?
RALEIGH. Baptist. I've been baptized. Don't have to keep being saved.
MAY. It's not exactly like that.
RALEIGH. A person doesn't have to stand up every time they hear the call, every time they hear "Lamb of God".
MAY. I don't.
RALEIGH. I never understood why people get saved all over again every summer.
MAY. I guess they have to, after the Nibroc festival. They go to the Nibroc festival, then they have to be saved again.
RALEIGH. You're wrong about that.

MAY. It just seems to me.
RALEIGH. The festival's not like that. Some people, some boys get a little moonshine, maybe, but it's mostly just to get people together. And elect the queen. The queen of the festival. It's like a fair.
MAY. I know what it's like.
RALEIGH. No, you don't. You haven't been.
MAY. I'm from Corbin. I know what the Nibroc festival is. You're not from Corbin. You don't know.
RALEIGH. I've been, though. I've been to the festival. And I'm going to take you to the festival.
MAY. No, you're not.
RALEIGH. Yes, I am. Next year I am going to take you to the Nibroc festival.
MAY. I thought you were going to New York City. *(A pause.)*
RALEIGH. I'm going to New York City and then I'm going to take you to the Nibroc festival.
MAY. If you go to New York City you won't be coming home to take me anywhere. People who go away, change. They're not like from home anymore.
RALEIGH. Like your fiancé.
MAY. Like him. Yes, like him.
RALEIGH. I was in California, too.
MAY. Well, I didn't know you before.
RALEIGH. You're starting to know me now.
MAY. We're just riding this train together. That's all. *(May starts reading her book. A pause.)*
RALEIGH. There aren't any other seats that I can see, but if I catch sight of anyone getting off at the next station I'll try to move.
MAY. You don't have to.
RALEIGH. I don't like to sit where I'm not welcome. I'll move just as soon as I can and some woman with a wailing baby will take my place. Well, I'm going to go ride back with the coffins. With F. Scott and Nathanael West.
MAY. Don't be silly.
RALEIGH. Is that a smile? No, couldn't be. Yep, I'd better go ride back there with the writers. The dead writers.
MAY. Stop.
RALEIGH. Old F. Scott and young Nat.

MAY. That's morbid.
RALEIGH. Scotty and Natty.
MAY. *(Suppressing a giggle in spite of herself.)* Scotty and Natty?
RALEIGH. Well, now. You're going home. See, you should be happy. Another few hours and you can change trains for Kentucky.
MAY. You, too.
RALEIGH. Nope. I'm staying. On the train. Going to New York City. Funny, when I got on, boarded the train, back in Los Angelees, I was going home. Not happy about it, but going home. I got on this train. Thought, I can go anywhere. Chicago, anywhere. No one's expecting me. No one knows I'm coming. Got a uniform still on, got a pass. Anywhere I want to go.
MAY. Well, I could go anywhere, too.
RALEIGH. You wanting to?
MAY. I don't know. Hadn't thought about it.
RALEIGH. Well, I have. I can go anywhere. Thought about Detroit, lots of work in the factories there, my brother-in-law says, but I can go do that any time.
MAY. You don't want to go home?
RALEIGH. Nope. Home'll always be there. I got on this train, and the conductor told me that the coffins were being loaded in. That Nathaniel West and F. Scott Fitzgerald were riding the same train I was. So, don't you see, I can't let that go by. When would something like that ever happen again?
MAY. You didn't know them.
RALEIGH. I didn't know you, either, but now we're riding the same train. And no matter what happens, there will always have been a time that we rode the train together. Things are affected by other things. And I can't let that go by. That I'm on the train with the two greatest writers of this century. And I thought I've just got to stay on this train. Follow those men. This is my chance, my time, and if I don't take it now, don't move right now, not later, now, while I'm supposed to, it'll never happen again.
MAY. But you didn't know them.
RALEIGH. Sure I know them! I know everything they've written. Feels like I know them better than I know myself, even. And something real deep inside — I don't usually just spill everything out like this. *(A pause.)* I know your feller. Your fiancé. *(May stares at*

him.) Not well, but I know him. I've seen your picture. He didn't get leave. I had to stay. To get ready to be discharged. My buddies got leave. For Christmas. I had to stay for processing.
MAY. They got time off?
RALEIGH. They got leave.
MAY. And he didn't?
RALEIGH. Reckon not.
MAY. How come?
RALEIGH. Must not've earned it. Must not've worked hard enough.
MAY. So I had to miss Christmas with my family? So I had to come all the way out here because he's lazy?
RALEIGH. I really don't know. Maybe he wanted you to come because he thought you've have a good time.
MAY. Well, he was wrong. I had a terrible time. He was different and he smoked and he didn't have any place for me to stay.
RALEIGH. Housing is getting tight, hard to —
MAY. Why'd he have me come out?
RALEIGH. Don't know. I don't know him very well.
MAY. And I slept on this porch, this woman's porch. Didn't really sleep, couldn't sleep, it was a porch. A porch in a strange place.
RALEIGH. Were you cold?
MAY. No, but it was just a porch.
RALEIGH. Don't you sleep on the porch back home? When it's hot?
MAY. Well, yes.
RALEIGH. A porch is a porch.
MAY. This was in a stranger's house. Not even the house. The porch. This woman I didn't know.
RALEIGH. Well, where did you want to sleep? A hotel?
MAY. Of course not! Not unless we, if we were —
RALEIGH. Were you planning to get married? Out there?
MAY. I don't know! It seemed — I just went because he — I don't know. And then it just wasn't the same. He's different.
RALEIGH. Everyone's different. Everyone's changing. The world's changed. You've changed.
MAY. You never knew me.
RALEIGH. No, but I'll just bet you've changed. Going all the way

across the country on a train. Something's got to be different when you get back. *(A pause.)* You gonna need my handkerchief again?
MAY. No, I'm not.
RALEIGH. It's here if you need it.
MAY. I don't.
RALEIGH. Well, just in case, it's here.
MAY. I wouldn't take your hanky if this train went through the Johnstown flood.
RALEIGH. Little missy, this trip of yours has sure made you feisty. Bet they won't even know you back in Corbin. You'll march into the Dixie Dog and they'll hand you the catsup without you even asking.
MAY. He's the one changed.
RALEIGH. Think so?
MAY. Know so.
RALEIGH. So. *(An uncomfortable pause.)*
MAY. I'm going to read now. If you don't mind.
RALEIGH. Be my guest. Back to your *Magnificent Obsession.*
MAY. Don't tell me the ending.
RALEIGH. You'll have to find out for yourself. *(Raleigh starts to stand up.)*
MAY. Going to the smoking car?
RALEIGH. That's right.
MAY. Don't come back smelling of smoke.
RALEIGH. I don't smoke.
MAY. In that case maybe I'll save your seat.
RALEIGH. Thanks. I'd like that. *(Raleigh turns to go up the aisle.)*
MAY. Wait. What did he say about me?
RALEIGH. Your feller? He said you were a goody two-shoes.
MAY. *(Pause.)* You think I'm a goody two-shoes?
RALEIGH. I think you think you are.
MAY. That's the same thing.
RALEIGH. Nope. I think deep down inside you have an adventurous spirit. Not every girl from Corbin, Kentucky, would get on a train and ride all the way to California not knowing what she was going to find there. Not many girls would talk to a soldier she didn't even know and cry in his handkerchief.
MAY. I'm going to be a missionary.

RALEIGH. Excuse me?
MAY. I told him. I've always wanted to be a missionary. He knew that. I wanted us to be missionaries.
RALEIGH. I said you had an adventurous spirit.
MAY. That's not adventurous.
RALEIGH. You don't like sleeping on a porch. Think you're going to like living in a hut?
MAY. I won't sleep in a hut.
RALEIGH. You sure will. Missionaries live in huts.
MAY. I hadn't thought about it.
RALEIGH. I reckon you hadn't thought about it. Well, you better be thinking about it. Think you were going to live on a plantation with native servants?
MAY. Not exactly.
RALEIGH. Doesn't your church pack up barrels with used clothes for the missionaries?
MAY. Well, yes.
RALEIGH. You'd be getting a barrel full of old clothes to hang up in your hut. It's a hard life for a woman.
MAY. I live on a farm. I can hoe a row, shuck corn, milk a cow and wring a chicken's neck.
RALEIGH. And I had you pegged for a town girl.
MAY. Just outside of town. Off highway twenty-five.
RALEIGH. North or south?
MAY. North.
RALEIGH. T'wards London.
MAY. Yes. Off twenty-five.
RALEIGH. You know the Logans?
MAY. Live across the road. They're neighbors.
RALEIGH. Cousins. I'm cousins with them. I know your farm. Nice piece of land.
MAY. It's —
RALEIGH. Not bottom land, like Raccoon Creek, but not too hilly.
MAY. We've got lots of blackberries.
RALEIGH. I love blackberries.
MAY. Me, too.
RALEIGH. I'll come pick blackberries on your farm and we'll go to the Nibroc Festival. Unless you're off in some jungle converting

the natives.
MAY. That will be a while. I just finished school. In Wilmore.
RALEIGH. Asbury College. Church school. So you're serious about this missionary work.
MAY. Of course I am.
RALEIGH. I thought you were just making it up.
MAY. Oh, no. I've been serious about it for a long time. I'm serious. I think.
RALEIGH. You think? You'd better think. It must be a hard life. Lonely. No one you know around. Nobody to speak your language with. Except a husband. *(A pause.)* You have to be married to be a missionary, don't you?
MAY. I think so.
RALEIGH. So, it'll be a while before you go away.
MAY. I suspect so.
RALEIGH. Why don't you come with me to New York City?
MAY. Excuse me?
RALEIGH. Come to New York City.
MAY. I don't know anyone in New York City.
RALEIGH. You know me. There's women's boarding houses. I've read about them.
MAY. Maybe you read too much.
RALEIGH. Maybe.
MAY. I could never live in a city.
RALEIGH. Have you ever been to one?
MAY. Silly. I just came from Los Angelees.
RALEIGH. That's not a real city.
MAY. I've been to Louisville [pronounced "L'LL-v'lle"]. I don't like Louisville.
RALEIGH. I wanted to go to Paris. With the war. And London. That's why I volunteered. London, England, not Kentucky. So if I can't go to Europe I'll go to New York City.
MAY. Well, I'm going home to Kentucky. And so should you.
RALEIGH. I'm going to New York City. Going to be a writer. When I'm a writer then I can go back home.
MAY. It won't be the same.
RALEIGH. It's not the same now. We're all changing. We're all riding this country's future like this train's a'rolling along the track,

just hoping we get somewhere and don't run off the tracks somewhere along the way. Trusting that the engineer and the brakeman and the signalman are all on the job, trusting that they'll get us there in one piece.
MAY. That's very poetic.
RALEIGH. Told you I was a writer.
MAY. So you did.
RALEIGH. Now prove to me that you're a missionary. Pray something for us. Pray that we get to where we're supposed to go. Pray that we don't go to war.
MAY. I'm having a hard time praying these days.
RALEIGH. Okay. I'll leave you alone. *(A pause.)*
MAY. I'm sorry I said those things.
RALEIGH. Which things are you sorry you said?
MAY. Well, about the porch. It wasn't so bad.
RALEIGH. Those things.
MAY. You keep teasing me.
RALEIGH. Just looking for the brighter side. *(A pause.)* Come to New York City.
MAY. With you? I don't do things like that.
RALEIGH. There's lady's boarding houses in New York City. Lots of jobs.
MAY. No. I'm not ... brave.
RALEIGH. You're very brave.
MAY. I'm not at all brave. I'm a scaredy cat. I'm a whipped pup, going home with my tail between my legs. I'm silly. I'm timid. I'm not at all brave.
RALEIGH. I think you're brave.
MAY. 'Cause I want to be a missionary?
RALEIGH. Wanting something's not brave. If you become a missionary, I reckon that would be brave, but giving it up is brave, too. Giving up one dream for another is brave. Oh, you gotta read Nathanael West. Everyday-ordinary things are brave sometimes. Talking to strangers like me is brave. Going to California took courage, and leaving it took even more.
MAY. I hadn't thought about it. I've mostly just been feeling bad.
RALEIGH. You should feel good about, well, about escaping that fate.

MAY. Is going to New York City brave?
RALEIGH. Of course it is!
MAY. Being a soldier is brave.
RALEIGH. Not being a soldier, flyer, is braver.
MAY. Why aren't you gonna be a flyer any more?
RALEIGH. Discharge. Medical discharge.
MAY. Why? *(A pause.)*
RALEIGH. I started getting the fits out there. *(May stares at him.)* Something sort of like the fits. Just a little bit. Once or twice only. But they're discharging me.
MAY. That's why you don't want to go home. *(A very long pause as May doesn't quite know what to say.)* You can always go to New York City later, if you really want to.
RALEIGH. But now's my opportunity.
MAY. Following dead men. Going to New York City because there's some dead men going there?
RALEIGH. They're famous writers.
MAY. They *were* famous writers, or so you say. I've never heard of one of them.
RALEIGH. He's famous.
MAY. But they're dead.
RALEIGH. They're famous writers.
MAY. But they're dead. It's over for them. Not you. Having a couple of little fits won't kill you. So why're you following dead men? Can't visit them in New York City. And are those coffins even going to New York? Isn't your friend Mr. Fitzgerald going to Virginia or Delaware or someplace?
RALEIGH. Maryland.
MAY. See? What'd he write about, anyway?
RALEIGH. Rich people, flappers.
MAY. Rich people where?
RALEIGH. The Riviera and New York City and —
MAY. He wrote about New York City.
RALEIGH. Yep.
MAY. So what are you going to write about?
RALEIGH. Stories.
MAY. About what?
RALEIGH. People.

MAY. People where?
RALEIGH. In the mountains.
MAY. In Kentucky.
RALEIGH. Yep.
MAY. So why are you going to New York City if you're going to write about Kentucky? *(Raleigh is taken aback. A pause.)*
RALEIGH. That's where writers go. New York City.
MAY. Are they happy there? You think Mr. Fitzgerald was happy in New York City?
RALEIGH. No.
MAY. Were you happy in Kentucky? You miss it?
RALEIGH. Yes, of course.
MAY. I don't have to say any more.
RALEIGH. No, I reckon you don't, little miss.
MAY. Excuse me, mister.
RALEIGH. My mistake. Taking this seat.
MAY. You can tease the dog but you don't like its bark. *(A long pause. Raleigh looks at May for a moment.)*
RALEIGH. Yes, I do. Like its bark. *(A pause.)* My name's Raleigh. Nice to meet you.
MAY. *(Offering her hand.)* Oh. I'm May. Nice to meet you.
RALEIGH. Well, May, I've got a question for you.
MAY. What is it?
RALEIGH. Well, if I come back to Kentucky —
MAY. When?
RALEIGH. Now. If I change trains with you, when you do —
MAY. You thinking about it?
RALEIGH. I'm thinking about it.
MAY. *(Teasing.)* It'd be a brave thing to do. Going to Kentucky. Brave.
RALEIGH. That's enough.
MAY. Sorry.
RALEIGH. As I was saying, May —
MAY. Yes, Raleigh.
RALEIGH. You got a mouth on you, you know.
MAY. Never had before. Guess I got too much sun in California.
RALEIGH. Well, anyway, if I go to Kentucky …
MAY. Yes.

RALEIGH. Hush, now, I want to say this.
MAY. All right.
RALEIGH. No, hush. *(A pause.)* I know you're just getting over, that you don't know. I mean about the missionary work — that you'll be, well, I reckon, do you — if I come home, haven't decided yet, mind you, but if I do, or when — Could I take you to the Nibroc festival?
MAY. Ask me when you're home.
RALEIGH. No, *now,* say I'm going home. I mean, say that's home, say that's where I'm going. Will you go to the Nibroc festival with me?
MAY. *(Pause.)* No. *(A long pause.)*
RALEIGH. Why not?
MAY. It's heathen.
RALEIGH. What? What do you mean?
MAY. People probably drinking. And dances. And beauty contests.
RALEIGH. That's heathen?
MAY. Well, no, but its name.
RALEIGH. Nibroc?
MAY. After some heathen god or something.
RALEIGH. What do you mean? It's not named after —
MAY. Or something heathen.
RALEIGH. Nibroc is Corbin spellt backwards.
MAY. No.
RALEIGH. Spell it out.
MAY. I never knew that. I never thought about it before. I never went.
RALEIGH. It's just a big party, May.
MAY. Funny how you grow up with things — .
RALEIGH. Yeah. Funny.
MAY. You come back to Kentucky and I'll go to the Nibroc festival with you.
RALEIGH. Really?
MAY. Yes, I'll go. But I won't go alone.
RALEIGH. I should think not. Well, then, maybe I'll just have to take you.
MAY. What about your friends in the coffins back there?
RALEIGH. They're "different from you and me." *(Blackout.)*

SCENE TWO

Late summer, just over a year and a half later — August 1942. At the edge of a large park. The cover on the train seat has been removed, revealing a park bench. A church bell chimes eight o'clock. Music is heard from a distance. May enters quickly and angrily, looking back over her shoulder. She sees the bench, starts to leave the other way, looks behind her again, and finally sits. She pulls a small bank bag out of her purse; the coins contained make a noise. She looks over her shoulder, then puts the bank bag under the bench, thinks better of it and retrieves it, getting up to try to find another hiding place. Out of frustration she finally throws it off stage as hard as she can. She listens for a bit and then sits on the bench, staring out. She folds her hands and bows her head, praying simply, as she does every night. This comforts her. Raleigh enters carrying the bag. He is wearing a plaid shirt and overalls, worn but clean and pressed. He stares at her praying for a moment. She finishes and looks out again, not seeing Raleigh. He jingles the bag of coins. She looks at him, startled.

RALEIGH. Not much of a festival this year.
MAY. You!
RALEIGH. Expecting somebody else? *(Raleigh and May just look at each other.)*
MAY. *(Shaken.)* Haven't seen you in over a year and you just appear like a ghost!
RALEIGH. Didn't mean to scare you.
MAY. Where'd you come from?
RALEIGH. *(Simply.)* Woodbine.
MAY. Where'd you come from just now?
RALEIGH. The judging tent. Them jelly's not much good. Not much good with so little sugar. Not much to taste. Not much to

25

judge. No, sir, not much of a Nibroc festival this year. It's a real disappointment so far.
MAY. Is it?
RALEIGH. Seen you at the judging tent. Did you taste them pickles?
MAY. You following me?
RALEIGH. Yep. Reckon we both are. Me and the preacher feller. You and the preacher fellow taste them pickles at the judging tent? Sure made me pucker up.
MAY. He's not following me.
RALEIGH. Never minded rationing before. Never missed the sugar 'til I tried them pickles just now.
MAY. I didn't try them.
RALEIGH. That was a wise decision.
MAY. I've got to get back. *(May takes the bag from Raleigh. A pause.)*
RALEIGH. Gonna be a nice twilight.
MAY. Could be.
RALEIGH. Yep, would've been nice weather for the big festival. If they'd held it. Not this rinky-dink little git-together.
MAY. You must have great expectations since you've been in the big city. Looking down on all us hillbillies back here.
RALEIGH. I just know what the festival used to be.
MAY. I wouldn't know.
RALEIGH. Didn't you go last year?
MAY. You know I didn't.
RALEIGH. I don't know anything. You mad at me?
MAY. I was.
RALEIGH. I figured you was.
MAY. Were.
RALEIGH. I figured you were. You didn't write back.
MAY. I didn't respond to one pitiful little postcard from Woodbine at Christmas time is what I didn't do. What I did do is start teaching school last fall in Lily, and keep on teaching Sunday School at Felt's Chapel, and learning to drive. I've been doing lots of things.
RALEIGH. You driving a car now?
MAY. How d'ya think I get to school?
RALEIGH. You got yourself a car?

MAY. Use my brother's. Got my own ration card for gasoline. He taught me to drive. I'm pretty good.
RALEIGH. I just bet you are. *(He looks at the bag and then off in the woods.)*
MAY. You see something? Somebody coming?
RALEIGH. Just a firefly.
MAY. Oh. Good.
RALEIGH. Why're you hiding from the preacher?
MAY. I'm not hiding. I'm just … I'm just taking a moment to myself.
RALEIGH. A moment to yourself.
MAY. To collect my thoughts a bit.
RALEIGH. To collect your thoughts.
MAY. And you're keeping me from doing just that.
RALEIGH. And I thought I was helping you.
MAY. Helping me? You helping me what?
RALEIGH. I told the preacher I seen you go the other way.
MAY. You did what?
RALEIGH. Told the preacher I seen you go the other way. *(May puts the money bag on the bench.)*
MAY. Saw. Saw me go the other way.
RALEIGH. *(Patiently.)* I told the preacher …
MAY. Why did you do that?
RALEIGH. Looked to me like you was trying to get away from him.
MAY. Were trying.
RALEIGH. *(Teasing her.)* Looked like you had an argument and you was trying to lose him. So when I seen you go this way, and he asked if I'd seen you, I said you went the other way. *(He smiles at her and shifts the bank bag on the bench.)*
MAY. Saw. It's *saw*, not *seen*.
RALEIGH. *(Playing with her.)* When he asked if I'd *saw* you …
MAY. *(Playing back at him.)* Seen.
RALEIGH. *(Feigning ignorance.)* You just said it was *saw*.
MAY. When you *saw* me.
RALEIGH. When I *saw* you.
MAY. He asked if you'd *seen*.
RALEIGH. He asked if I'd *seen* you. And I said I seen you go off the other way.

MAY. Saw. *(Trying not to laugh.)*
RALEIGH. *(Tongue-in-cheek.)* I said you were gone.
MAY. *(Laughing.)* Why would you do that?
RALEIGH. Looked like you wanted to be gone. So I helped you out.
MAY. I don't need any help from you. What time is it?
RALEIGH. Little after eight. *(May stands up quickly, as if to go.)* Want me to go fetch him for you?
MAY. No.
RALEIGH. Want me to deliver anything to him? *(Raleigh glances down at the bank bag.)* Something I might've found over yonder in the woods?
MAY. No.
RALEIGH. Want me to leave?
MAY. Yes.
RALEIGH. Need my handkerchief?
MAY. *(Emphatically.)* I don't need anybody's handkerchief. *(A pause.)*
RALEIGH. Reckon I'll be going then. Nice to *see* you. Glad I *saw* you.
MAY. Why'd you follow me?
RALEIGH. Wanted to *see* you again.
MAY. Why?
RALEIGH. Just wanted to, that's all.
MAY. Well, you have.
RALEIGH. Yep, I sure have. That's right. I sure have. I have *seen* you. You have *seen* me. We have *seen* each other. *(A slight pause.)* And you, you've been seeing the preacher. So what'ja running from the preacher for?
MAY. I reckon I don't know no more. *Any* more.
RALEIGH. You sure have turned into a school teacher.
MAY. I just hate to hear bad grammar. Especially from you. You were going to be a writer. You read lots of books. I liked hearing about all the books you read.
RALEIGH. I don't read much now. Not even the paper. Too much going on. Too much I'm missing out on. Can't join up, won't be drafted, can't even work on the line in the factory. Not much use reading books if I can't do anything. Can't afford 'em, anyway.

MAY. There's the library.
RALEIGH. I reckon.
MAY. You used to read big books and talk about ideas.
RALEIGH. Thought you didn't like them ol' ideas of mine.
MAY. Your grammar's gotten awful.
RALEIGH. Must be teaching school has made you listen to it diffcrent. Differently.
MAY. Must be. *(A pause.)* How was Detroit? I heard from somebody you went off to Detroit.
RALEIGH. Now don't tell me you've been asking around about me.
MAY. Sometimes people tell you things whether you care to hear it or not.
RALEIGH. Yep, sometimes people say things you don't want to hear.
MAY. You just up and left town.
RALEIGH. Figured you didn't want to see me.
MAY. You had dinner with my family. And then you up and left town.
RALEIGH. Now wait a minute. You was supposed to have dinner with my family.
MAY. You *were* supposed to have … Supper. It was going to be supper. So why aren't you in Detroit? I think you should be in Detroit. You belong in a city. Don't you like Detroit? What's the matter? Couldn't you keep a job?
RALEIGH. That's right.
MAY. I was just joking.
RALEIGH. No joke. I couldn't keep a job.
MAY. But there's lots of jobs there. Lots of factories. My brother says. Lots of jobs now.
RALEIGH. Not for me.
MAY. You must be pretty lazy not to keep a job. Why, they just hire anybody. From anywhere — there's foreigners there. They hire all kinds of people.
RALEIGH. Not me.
MAY. Couldn't work with the foreigners?
RALEIGH. People're people.
MAY. They're foreigners.
RALEIGH. What would you know about foreigners?

MAY. Seen one down t' the lumberyard. There's one working at the lumberyard. A foreigner. I said hello to him just last week. A foreigner.
RALEIGH. *(Amused.)* You'd 'ave made a good missionary, that's for sure! It's a good thing you haven't gone off into the world and become a missionary. The whole world may go to war, but at least it'll be safe from you.
MAY. That's a mean thing to say.
RALEIGH. Sorry. Just made me laugh for a minute.
MAY. Glad it's funny to you. 'Cause it's serious to me. There's plenty of missionary work to do right here.
RALEIGH. I just bet there is. Lots of missionary work. You gonna help out your preacher friend with his mission work? *(He looks at May, who doesn't answer.)* I heard you and the preacher feller were getting serious. Heard he was walking you home from the revival meetings.
MAY. You hear a lot.
RALEIGH. Not enough. Tell me, how does he keep so slick looking if he's always kneeling in the sawdust saving people?
MAY. He's a good dresser. Sets an example.
RALEIGH. Snappy-looking, all right.
MAY. He keeps himself tidy.
RALEIGH. Summer's almost over. Festival's over. Tent meeting's over. He's off to someplace else tomorrow.
MAY. I reckon so.
RALEIGH. He ask you to go with him?
MAY. You think you know everything, don't you?
RALEIGH. He ask you to go with him?
MAY. Yes, he did.
RALEIGH. You going?
MAY. I don't know what I'm going to do. He wants us to be missionaries.
RALEIGH. Well, that's what you always wanted. I don't see any difficulties here.
MAY. He's leaving on the train tonight. I'm supposed to meet him at the train station.
RALEIGH. Never know what'll happen on a train. Might as well go. Sounds like a pretty good offer to me.

MAY. Things aren't always as easy as you make 'em out to be.
RALEIGH. I never said things were easy. I'm back in town now. You think that's easy?
MAY. What's so hard about it? It's where you're from. You keep coming and going so much how can a'body keep track of you?
RALEIGH. You better get going if you're going to catch the evening train.
MAY. I reckon so.
RALEIGH. Is he your "magnificent obsession," May? You in love with the preacher? *(A pause. May looks away as if she's about to cry.)*
RALEIGH. *(Tenderly.)* What's the matter, Maisy? Did he make advances to you? Did he try to hurt you?
MAY. No, he never, he'd never do a thing like that. You just don't know anything, do you?
RALEIGH. Not if you don't tell me.
MAY. I don't want to talk about it.
RALEIGH. May, what'd he do? *(May doesn't answer.)* Just tell me. You should tell me.
MAY. I was helping him count the offering.
RALEIGH. He's stealing the offering?
MAY. No. I don't know. Every night I've been helping him. Count the money. It goes to the church. And for the use of the campground.
RALEIGH. Sounds reasonable.
MAY. But every night he puts away a few dollars for "his expenses."
RALEIGH. Still sounds reasonable.
MAY. But if he's a true missionary, all that money should go back to the church. Not to him.
RALEIGH. He's got to have some traveling money.
MAY. And then tonight he kept all of the money. For his expenses. If he were a true man of God he'd just trust that God was feeding him and looking out for him. That's what I would do. If he'd been a true man of God, he'd have trusted that God was providing for him.
RALEIGH. God did provide for him. He provided a lot of people and a big offering at the last meeting so the preacher would have enough money to get to the next town.
MAY. You've changed.

RALEIGH. So've you.
MAY. If I may say so, you have become very narrow-minded.
RALEIGH. *(Laughs.)* You may not say so, and you are even more narrow-minded. You'll make quite a missionary. *(A pause.)* May, why didn't you come over and have supper with my family last year?
MAY. I just changed my mind, that's all. Person's allowed to change their mind.
RALEIGH. Person's allowed. Person's gotta have a reason, though.
MAY. Just changed my mind.
RALEIGH. 'Cause I whooped your brother for hiding in the back seat of the Rambler?
MAY. You were just playing.
RALEIGH. 'Cause I argued with your daddy about Roosevelt?
MAY. He loves talk, "to debate current issues," as he calls it.
RALEIGH. Must've been you and me then. Must've been me and you. And I thought we were getting along so well.
MAY. We were. Wasn't you.
RALEIGH. What, then? You hadn't met the preacher then.
MAY. That why you followed me just now? To ask me why I didn't have supper with you over a year ago? Over a year ago, before you went off to Detroit and never wrote me.
RALEIGH. I sent you a postcard.
MAY. Not much of a writer, are you?
RALEIGH. *(After a beat.)* I reckon I'm not. Not anymore, anyway.
MAY. I'm sorry I said that. My mouth just seems to run away from me sometimes these days. *(A pause.)*
RALEIGH. Mind if I set a spell?
MAY. Don't make no nevermind to me.
RALEIGH. Don't want to intrude.
MAY. Sure you got better places to be. With your friends.
RALEIGH. Tired of them. All they talk about is when they'll go to war. When they'll be drafted. Should they join up. They're not much fun. Rather be settin' here with you.
MAY. I'm not much fun.
RALEIGH. Maybe not. But you're prettier. Why didn't you come to supper at our place last year? *(May doesn't answer.)* I had dinner with your family. Went to Felt's Chapel and then Sunday dinner.
MAY. I remember.

RALEIGH. Your mom's a good cook.
MAY. I helped with the soup beans. Snapped the beans.
RALEIGH. It was a real good dinner.
MAY. Wasn't anything special.
RALEIGH. Your family's real nice.
MAY. They were on good behavior. For the most part. They were on their best behavior. Except for my brother Charlie. And my Daddy liked talking with you. Thought you were real bright.
RALEIGH. But I wanted to be with you.
MAY. I had to help clean up.
RALEIGH. Wanted to take a drive with you. Had my uncle's Rambler that night.
MAY. Well, we tried.
RALEIGH. That son-of-a-gun brother of yours.
MAY. Charlie thought it was funny. Won't let me live it down yet. The family's still talking about it.
RALEIGH. Him a'hiding. Hiding in the back seat of the Rambler.
MAY. You sure scared him on the turns.
RALEIGH. No.
MAY. Don't you remember?
RALEIGH. He got carsick. Don't you remember? That's why he had to get off the back floor.
MAY. He got carsick because of those turns. Up the mountain.
RALEIGH. That's when he popped his head up.
MAY. You liked to run off the road when you saw his face in the mirror.
RALEIGH. I knew he was there. That's why I was taking the turns so fast.
MAY. You didn't know anything of the kind.
RALEIGH. Did, too. That's why I was driving up the mountain.
MAY. You were driving up the mountain to get me alone.
RALEIGH. I was driving up the mountain to shake up your little brother.
MAY. You were driving too fast. You still drive that fast?
RALEIGH. I don't drive any more.
MAY. Shouldn't use gasoline if you don't have to.
RALEIGH. Sure did scare your brother, though. He was really

carsick.
MAY. I was so mad at him.
RALEIGH. I was, too.
MAY. I bet you were. He ruined all your plans.
RALEIGH. What plans you talking 'bout, May?
MAY. To get me alone top the mountain, that's what.
RALEIGH. What makes you think I had plans like that?
MAY. Why else'd you be driving me up there?
RALEIGH. See the moon, maybe.
MAY. And the stars. Don't forget the stars.
RALEIGH. That's right.
MAY. I recollect it was cloudy.
RALEIGH. All I recollect is how pretty you looked. *(They look at each other for a while.)* Come have supper with my folks. Won't you?
MAY. Can't. I can't. Charlie says ... Did I tell you? He just joined up. *(A pause.)*
RALEIGH. No. He's not old enough.
MAY. Just barely. He joined up. Not the infantry. He's going to fly. He wants to learn to fly. So he joined up.
RALEIGH. Well, good for him. Hope he doesn't get carsick in the airplanes. Hope flying don't give him the fits.
MAY. You still get the fits?
RALEIGH. Sometimes.
MAY. I thought that was over. In California.
RALEIGH. It started in California. I thought it would go away. Came back in Detroit.
MAY. Working gives you the fits?
RALEIGH. Farm work doesn't. Seems like lights is what makes the fits come on. The airplanes have lights on them. Assembly line at the factory. Blinking lights. Seems like them lights is what makes the fits happen.
MAY. Those lights.
RALEIGH. What lights?
MAY. It's *those* lights, not *them* lights.
RALEIGH. You mad at me? Or you just fussin' at me right now because your preacher friend isn't here for you to be mad at.
MAY. Did you follow me out here to ask me about the preacher?
RALEIGH. Nope. My buddy made me a bet. He bet me a dollar

that you wouldn't even talk to me no more 'cause you were going with the preacher.
MAY. You followed me because you made a bet?
RALEIGH. Reckon I won it, too.
MAY. You started gambling now?
RALEIGH. It was just in fun.
MAY. Make bets a lot, do you?
RALEIGH. It was just a game.
MAY. Lose all your money in Detroit making bets?
RALEIGH. Sorry I mentioned it.
MAY. Guess it runs in the family.
RALEIGH. Guess what does?
MAY. Gambling, smoking, drinking.
RALEIGH. What are you talking about?
MAY. Gambling, smoking, and drinking. Just what don't you understand about that? Seems to me you understand it pretty well.
RALEIGH. You think I run around fast?
MAY. Your daddy does.
RALEIGH. My daddy's a cripple. He walks with two canes. He's a cripple.
MAY. From drinking. Your daddy's got Jake leg.
RALEIGH. He got that more'n ten years ago.
MAY. He's got Jake leg. My brother Charlie told me your daddy's got Jake leg. He got it drinking Jamaica gin. Everybody knows what causes Jake leg. *(A slight pause.)*
RALEIGH. So you won't come and sit down with my family because my daddy's a cripple?
MAY. That's not it.
RALEIGH. You won't eat supper with my daddy?
MAY. Your daddy's a drinker.
RALEIGH. Just because he didn't stick to moonshine like everyone else was doing back then.
MAY. My daddy didn't drink moonshine.
RALEIGH. Bet he did. Bet he made it, too. Just ask him for the recipe some day. Bet your daddy didn't have to use an old radiator, either. Bet he had real copper pipes. Your daddy didn't get paralyzed 'cause he was making moonshine himself or buying it from Buggytop Shelton.

MAY. How would you know about Buggytop Shelton?
RALEIGH. Same as you. Folks talk about things. Most are just not as mean about it as you are.
MAY. I'm not mean. I'm religious. *(Pause.)* D'you drink? D'you buy moonshine from Buggytop Shelton?
RALEIGH. No. But I bet if I'd been in Paris and London I'd've been drinking wine and gin and all the stuff they drink there. When there's a war you gotta drink.
MAY. There wasn't any war going on when your daddy got Jake leg. It was Prohibition, not a war.
RALEIGH. You're just judging everybody in sight, aren't you? Ought to be over yonder at the judging tent, judging those sour pickles. People make mistakes. Careful you don't make any mistakes. *(A pause.)* You going to cry?
MAY. I don't cry anymore.
RALEIGH. Reckon you don't have feelings anymore.
MAY. Reckon I don't. You going to have a fit?
RALEIGH. *(A slight pause.)* Reckon you don't have any feelings any more. Reckon it's better that way. One thing we can agree on, anyway. Not to have any feelings.
MAY. There's a war on.
RALEIGH. Reckon that's what's happened to our feelings. *(They sit in silence for a minute.)*
MAY. Charlie's going any week now. My mama just can't stop crying. Seems like if she cries I can't.
RALEIGH. I'm sorry, May. *(Pause.)* I wish I was going. Wish I could go in Charlie's place. In anybody's place. *(Pause.)* Just going to stay here and take care of my folks. Everybody wondering why I'm not going.
MAY. Everybody knows farmers get to stay. The preacher's going to raise onions so he doesn't have to go.
RALEIGH. Maybe you should just go help him. Raise some onions. Raise some pigs, too. Wring some chickens' necks. Maybe you should do some hard work.
MAY. I work hard. I work very hard.
RALEIGH. Teaching school.
MAY. I have fifty-one children in my classroom. Fifty-one. And don't think I don't use the paddle when I have to.

RALEIGH. I just bet you do.
MAY. I do.
RALEIGH. Glad I'm not in your class.
MAY. I'd use it on you.
RALEIGH. I bet you would.
MAY. Whenever you'd mouth off.
RALEIGH. I'd mouth off a lot with you.
MAY. Not in my class you wouldn't.
RALEIGH. Bet I would.
MAY. Bet I wouldn't let you.
RALEIGH. Bet you couldn't stop me.
MAY. Bet I could.
RALEIGH. Tell me how.
MAY. I'd paddle you.
RALEIGH. You wouldn't.
MAY. If I had to, I would. I'd paddle you.
RALEIGH. How you gonna catch me to paddle me?
MAY. I'd use a switch. Switch's longer. I'd use a switch on you.
RALEIGH. Where're you gonna get a switch?
MAY. Bushes back by the outhouse.
RALEIGH. You gonna go run out and cut a switch.
MAY. Switch'd reach you better'n a paddle would. Hurt more, too.
RALEIGH. By the time you'd cut a switch I'd be gone. Think I'm gonna sit on a milkin' stool in the corner waiting for you to go out to the outhouse and cut a switch?
MAY. I can run fast as you.
RALEIGH. What would you do when you catch up with me, then? What would you do, then? I'm too big for you to paddle. What would you do?
MAY. I'd tell you off.
RALEIGH. I can mouth off good as you.
MAY. I'd make you behave.
RALEIGH. What're you gonna do? Can't paddle me, can't outtalk me, what're you gonna do, May? Take away my toys? Take my belongings out of my book bag? Or out of my valise? *(A pause.)*
MAY. I wouldn't take your things.
RALEIGH. Wouldn't have thought a fine religious woman like you would take anything from anybody.

MAY. I wouldn't. *(May picks up the bank bag.)* I'm giving it back to the church.
RALEIGH. May, the man's gotta make a living. How's you two gonna live?
MAY. People take care of him. He lives in people's houses. They feed him.
RALEIGH. In the summer. What do you think he does when he's not making the tent circuit? How do you think you're gonna live?
MAY. Is he a friend of yours? One of your buddies? You sure are standing up for him an awful lot.
RALEIGH. I just see both sides of it.
MAY. You must like him. You must think he's a good person.
RALEIGH. Well, I don't think he's a bad person. Just a man trying to make a living, that's all. And, no, I don't like him. I don't like the way he dresses in that white suit, and I don't like the way he talks so kind and quiet like, and I don't like the way he guided your elbow when you walked through the crowd together at the judging tent. No, I don't like him. I don't like him at'll.
MAY. You watched us?
RALEIGH. Seen you.
MAY and RALEIGH. *(Together.) Saw.*
RALEIGH. *Saw* you. *(They just look at each other.)* How'd you get so prickly, May? Don't remember you being so prickly. A little feisty, maybe, but not prickly.
MAY. I'm just more grown up now.
RALEIGH. You're just more prickly now. Like a blackberry bush. Or a rose bush. You used to be a, a weeping willow, that's what you used to be, a weeping willow, but now you're just a prickly old blackberry bush. Gotta watch out for you. Don't want to get blackberry stains all over me. No, sir, blackberry stains're hard to wash out.
MAY. You can leave now.
RALEIGH. Think maybe I will.
MAY. You're just an old …
RALEIGH. An old what, May?
MAY. An old, an old tree. Won't move. An old tree. That won't move.
RALEIGH. Like one of those big old trees over yonder that rises so majestically from the ground?
MAY. Just an old tree.

RALEIGH. That shades and protects us? That awes us in the fall and takes our breath away in the spring?
MAY. You're always laughing at me.
RALEIGH. Not anymore, May.
MAY. You're just an old tree.
RALEIGH. Like one of those big old trees over t' the cemetery? Big old trees standing over the graves. Shading and protecting dead people? Yep, you're right. I feel just like one of those big old trees over t' the cemetery.
MAY. You're an old dead tree.
RALEIGH. Or maybe I'm an old dead tree that's been uprooted by a big tornado, lying on its side with all its roots exposed to the howling wind and the pouring rain. Yep, reckon you're right about something, May. I'm just an old dead tree. Reckon I'm gonna be a stump soon. Just a stump in the ground, so you can sit on me. When you teach them fifty screaming kids of yours about trees, you can tell them what a stump I am. Just a blackberry-stained stump with you a'sittin' on me. *(A pause.)*
MAY. You trying to be poetical? I'd give that a low mark in my class.
RALEIGH. You don't have to grade me, May. I can do it myself. Give myself the low marks. Don't need you to do it for me.
MAY. Then I don't have to bother with you, then.
RALEIGH. You got that right. You sure got that right, missy. You don't have to bother with me no more, any more, missy. Missy Maisy. And I'm sorry I followed you here. Sorry I told the preacher you went the other way. Sorry you've become so prickly. Sorry I ever rode a train with you.
MAY. I'm sorry, too.
RALEIGH. Then we're both pretty sorry.
MAY. I'm leaving now.
RALEIGH. I'm leaving now, too. Want me to walk you to the train station?
MAY. No. And don't follow me again, neither.
RALEIGH. Wouldn't dream of it.
MAY. I'm leaving.
RALEIGH. So'm I. *(A pause.)* You're not leaving very fast.
MAY. I reckon I'm just not a very nice person sometimes.
RALEIGH. If you're wanting me to agree with you, it's not all

that hard right now.
MAY. I'm sorry about your daddy. And I'm sorry I took the preacher's money. I feel sort of ashamed.
RALEIGH. You don't know what being ashamed is.
MAY. I feel very ashamed.
RALEIGH. Ashamed is when you can't go off to war with your buddies. When you're going to be the only one left in town.
MAY. *(Almost overlapping.)* I know that.
RALEIGH. Ashamed is when you have the fits in front of your sergeant.
MAY. *(Almost overlapping.)* I'm sure it is.
RALEIGH. Ashamed is when you give up your own dreams to chase after something in a skirt and find out she's not worth running after.
MAY. You're not talking about me.
RALEIGH. Ashamed is when your new girl won't come to supper at your house because your daddy is a cripple.
MAY. I said I was sorry —
RALEIGH. Ashamed is when you run into that girl a year and half later and you realize what a stupid mule-headed old rooster you've been for ever seeing something in her in the first place. Ashamed is having to come home to a dirt-poor farm and feeling guilty about taking care of your mama and your daddy. And instead of going off to war having to go to Detroit to stand fifteen hours a day on the line in a loud, sweaty dark factory. Ashamed is when the factory doctor tells you you got ep'lepsy.
MAY. You preaching at me? *(He is having the very beginnings of very mild convulsions.)*
RALEIGH. You better leave now. Better catch your train.
MAY. Are you all right? You need a handkerchief? Raleigh, you all right? I'll get someone to help.
RALEIGH. It's just a fit. It's the ep'lepsy.
MAY. *(Scared.)* They put people away for having fits.
RALEIGH. The factory doctor said it was ep'lepsy.
MAY. I'm so sorry, Raleigh. Really I am. Forgive me. *(He doesn't hear her. The clock strikes the half hour and May runs off. Raleigh's petit mal convulsions continue into the blackout.)*

SCENE THREE

The following spring — May 1943. Early evening. The park bench has now become a chintz-covered porch settee or a swing. Perhaps a flag hangs from the window behind it, with a star on it. Raleigh enters from the house, looking older and a little sad. He pulls a brown paper bag out from under the porch seat and and holds it, staring out. He changes his mind and puts back on the floor under the settee. May enters from the house. She looks tired and more mature. They stare out in silence for a moment.

MAY. Sure is bright down there. Never seen the sky so bright at night. Not even with a full moon. *(Pause.)* Why's it so bright?
RALEIGH. Lumberyard. Lumberyard's burning.
MAY. I know. But why does it burn so bright? Seems like it shoulda burned itself out by now.
RALEIGH. It's a lumberyard.
MAY. Seems the wood 'a burn itself out quickly.
RALEIGH. Big storehouse at the lumberyard.
MAY. Seems it would burn quickly, then. All that wood.
RALEIGH. Lots of paint. And glue.
MAY. I forgot about that.
RALEIGH. Those kinda things real flammable.
MAY. Oh, of course.
RALEIGH. Just gotta burn itself out.
MAY. Seems like they shoulda put it out by now. Everybody down there helping. Can't they put out the fire?
RALEIGH. Not with all that paint and glue a'burning.
MAY. They're just gonna watch it burn?
RALEIGH. Just keep it from spreading. Just contain the fire. It's too hot to fight.
MAY. I wish it would rain. That would put it out.
RALEIGH. Gotta burn itself out. Nothing anybody can do. It's

too hot.
MAY. Sure makes the sky real bright.
RALEIGH. Sure does.
MAY. Sure is bright.
RALEIGH. Sure is.
MAY. It's kinda pretty. *(Raleigh doesn't answer.)* Reckon that's what the war looks like? The sky all lit up like that?
RALEIGH. Could be.
MAY. Never thought the war could look pretty.
RALEIGH. Reckon sometimes it seems to.
MAY. Wonder if that's what the sky looked like to Charlie. When he was parachuting down. Wonder if it was all lit up like that.
RALEIGH. Probably even brighter.
MAY. Sure is burning bright. *(A long pause, while they watch the sky.)*
RALEIGH. If you want to drive down and see it, go ahead.
MAY. I don't like to drive at night.
RALEIGH. I'm on a bicycle.
MAY. I know. You want to go down there?
RALEIGH. Too many people. I don't like being around people much these days.
MAY. I don't want to go down there, anyway. *(Raleigh sits beside her.)*
RALEIGH. That was a good dinner.
MAY. Not bad with the rationing goin' on.
RALEIGH. Wouldn't even know it.
MAY. I'm so tired of cornbread, aren't you? Wish we could have had biscuits.
RALEIGH. I thought it was a real good dinner. I appreciate it.
MAY. Least I could do.
RALEIGH. Didn't have to do anything.
MAY. Well, actually, Mama made most of the dinner. I just helped with some of the vegetables.
RALEIGH. It was real nice.
MAY. I'm not much of a cook. Never learned to cook much.
RALEIGH. I thought it was all real tasty. It was a real nice dinner. Good of you to invite me. *(A pause.)*
MAY. I am so sorry about my daddy running on so. He always does after a glass of sherry. *(They share a look.)* He just loves to talk about

all the news. I'm surprised he had the radio off during supper. Just talk, talk, talk. Talk about the battles. Talk about Europe. Talk about the Pacific. He can't talk about anything but the war. Can't seem to get enough of it.
RALEIGH. Nice to see him again.
MAY. He sure likes arguing with you. But he does run on. Especially during supper time.
RALEIGH. Well, I sure appreciated the fine meal. And the good company.
MAY. Hard to cook with the rationing on.
RALEIGH. I'm not much for sweets.
MAY. Thanks for bringing the strawberries.
RALEIGH. They're good this year.
MAY. Yes, they are. *(Silence.)*
RALEIGH. Reckon I should be leaving, then. Got a train to catch tomorrow. *(A pause.)*
MAY. You're leaving town?
RALEIGH. That's right.
MAY. When?
RALEIGH. Tomorrow. *(A pause.)*
MAY. Going back to Detroit?
RALEIGH. New York City.
MAY. Why?
RALEIGH. Nothing for me here.
MAY. You're going to New York City? On the train? Tomorrow?
RALEIGH. That's right. Came to say good-bye. *(Raleigh stands up. May is speechless.)* Don't want to keep you. I reckon you have t' get up pretty early.
MAY. You gotta go so soon? We haven't had a chance to catch up.
RALEIGH. Not much to catch up on. You still teaching, I reckon. *(A pause.)*
MAY. Oh, I didn't get to tell you. I didn't get to tell you a thing. I'm principal now. Over t' Paint Lick High School. I'm principal now.
RALEIGH. Is that right?
MAY. They made me the principal. Funny times we're living in. I just barely got outa school and they made me the principal.
RALEIGH. Must be hard.
MAY. I thought it would be. But it was more money. More

money'n teaching at Lilly. I thought it would be harder. But nothin's harder than fifty screaming children in one classroom.
RALEIGH. Teaching high school must be hard.
MAY. I thought it would be. But the boys, the really bad ones, they just join up in the service quick as they get old enough. Or even before if they can get away with it. One nice thing about the war. The boys get to go fight, so they don't have to do it at the school. Hard on the younger ones, though. Their brothers all sent off, sometimes their daddies, even. But the big boys, the bad ones are all gone. And the girls aren't much trouble. Always sewing, and writing letters and sending packages. We encourage them to write to the soldiers.
RALEIGH. So the girls aren't much trouble.
MAY. Never are. It's always the boys that are the trouble.
RALEIGH. *(With a twinkle in his eye.)* I beg to differ.
MAY. You're wrong. It's the boys that cause the problems. It's always the boys that are trouble.
RALEIGH. *(Laughing at her.)* I would have to differ with that statement.
MAY. Are you laughing at me? You always ... I'm telling you, it's the boys that make all the problems. It's the boys that fight. It's the boys that cause wars. It's the boys that go crazy. *(A pause.)* I'm sorry. I'm sorry I said "crazy." I meant they get mean. I didn't mean to say "crazy."
RALEIGH. It's all right, May. *(An uncomfortable pause.)*
MAY. I've been wanting to apologize.
RALEIGH. What for, May?
MAY. For things I said. Last time I saw you. For leaving you when the ambulance came.
RALEIGH. You already apologized for that.
MAY. In the letters.
RALEIGH. Apology's an apology.
MAY. I wanted to apologize in person.
RALEIGH. Apology already accepted, May.
MAY. You got all my letters? I wanted to make sure I wrote to you every week. Did you get one every week? While you were in the hospital?
RALEIGH. I recollect I did. I haven't gotten any since, though.

MAY. I wrote you every week.
RALEIGH. I've been home for three weeks. Haven't gotten a letter.
MAY. I kept meaning to write after I heard you were home.
RALEIGH. It was nice to get the letters.
MAY. I didn't know if anyone else would write you.
RALEIGH. My daddy can't hold a pen for long. Just to sign his name.
MAY. Your mama wrote you, didn't she? She told me she did.
RALEIGH. She's not much for writing. She appreciated your bringing the corn and the apples.
MAY. Nice that your sister's moved back.
RALEIGH. It's a real help. She and my mama came to visit. Took the bus every week.
MAY. I didn't know you could have visitors.
RALEIGH. You never asked.
MAY. You could've told me you could have visitors.
RALEIGH. It wasn't prison, May.
MAY. Don't they have bars on the windows?
RALEIGH. It's not a prison. Just a state hospital.
MAY. But they've got bars on the windows.
RALEIGH. Yes, May, they've got bars on the windows. *(A pause.)*
MAY. You want to talk about it?
RALEIGH. Nope.
MAY. It might be good to talk about it. With a friend.
RALEIGH. You my friend, May?
MAY. Well, of course, I am.
RALEIGH. I'm glad to know that.
MAY. And you're looking really good. I didn't expect you to look this good.
RALEIGH. I'm doing all right.
MAY. Your, well, your skin looks real good. Good color.
RALEIGH. My skin is fine.
MAY. Well, I'm so glad to hear that. So glad to hear that your skin is fine. *(A pause.)* I know I wasn't much of a friend. When you got sick at the festival. Not much of a friend to anybody. I was scared that night. He's overseas now. The preacher is. Army chaplain.
RALEIGH. Well, good for him.
MAY. He joined up.

RALEIGH. You write to him?
MAY. No. I don't.
RALEIGH. He write to you?
MAY. No. He doesn't.
RALEIGH. Well, good for him. Joining up, that is. Good for him. You write your other feller?
MAY. I don't have a boyfriend. I write to Charlie.
RALEIGH. Your feller you were engaged to. You write to him?
MAY. I never wrote to him after I came home.
RALEIGH. You never did?
MAY. No, I never did.
RALEIGH. He ever write to you?
MAY. When he got to England, he did. But I never wrote back.
RALEIGH. He still writing you?
MAY. He got killed.
RALEIGH. Shot down?
MAY. No. He was in an automobile accident. Goes to war to fly, but gets killed in a car.
RALEIGH. Sorry to hear that. He was a lot of fun.
MAY. He got killed. Glad I didn't marry him. I'd be a widow. That's a mean thing to say, isn't it.
RALEIGH. That's an honest thing to say.
MAY. *(A pause.)* I'm sorry I ran away from you that night.
RALEIGH. Reckon you got home all righty. In the dark and all.
MAY. I felt bad leaving you.
RALEIGH. I know.
MAY. I didn't know they'd keep you in the hospital.
RALEIGH. Wasn't anything you could have done.
MAY. You want to talk about it? Being in the crazy hospital?
RALEIGH. You want me to talk about it, May?
MAY. If you want to.
RALEIGH. I don't want to.
MAY. It helps to talk about things.
RALEIGH. I know it does.
MAY. To tell all about it.
RALEIGH. Yes, it helps to tell all about it.
MAY. I'm willing to listen. *(Raleigh doesn't answer.)* It helps to talk about it. Why, when Charlie was captured, when they brought the

telegram telling us he'd been shot down and captured, I just couldn't stop thinking about it and praying for him, and couldn't, well, couldn't think about anything at school and at all. Mama just kept crying, and I couldn't talk to her 'cause she'd just cry, and everybody at school had people missing or dead or something, so I didn't want to burden them. So I just wrote everything to you, like I was talking to you, and it helped. It helped an awful lot.
RALEIGH. I liked getting your letters.
MAY. So you see, it really helps to talk about it. Or write about it.
RALEIGH. I did write about it.
MAY. I didn't get any letters. Just a couple of postcards.
RALEIGH. I wrote about it for the newspapers. Sold it, too.
MAY. Sold what?
RALEIGH. The article I wrote. *(He pulls a newspaper clipping out of his shirt pocket and hands it to May.)*
MAY. *(Reading the title.)* "A Prisoner in My Own War." You wrote this?
RALEIGH. Wrote it.
MAY. Well, if that doesn't beat anything.
RALEIGH. Sold it. To the *Courier-Journal*.
MAY. My, that sure is something.
RALEIGH. I thought so. Wrote it in the hospital.
MAY. That's something to be proud of.
RALEIGH. I am. I'm right proud of that.
MAY. I should think so. What's it about?
RALEIGH. About being in the hospital. About being in a crazy hospital when you're not crazy.
MAY. Will you have to go back to the hospital?
RALEIGH. Not that hospital.
MAY. No, of course you wouldn't.
RALEIGH. 'Nother hospital maybe sometime. Regular hospital.
MAY. I'm sorry I didn't come visit. Was it awful?
RALEIGH. It was pretty bad.
MAY. I'm just so sorry.
RALEIGH. You keep saying that.
MAY. I don't know what else to say.
RALEIGH. There's nothing to say.
MAY. I guess not. *(A long, uncomfortable pause.)* You must've been

glad to be home. For a while, anyway.
RALEIGH. I was.
MAY. What have you been doing with yourself?
RALEIGH. Reading and writing.
MAY. Glad to hear you've been reading again. F. Scott Fitzgerald?
RALEIGH. Nope. Lloyd C. Douglas.
MAY. You're making fun of me.
RALEIGH. Nope. I've been reading Lloyd C. Douglas. Brought you something. *(Raleigh gets the brown paper bag and a business-size envelope from underneath the seat and hands both to her.)*
MAY. What's this about?
RALEIGH. Happy birthday, May.
MAY. You remembered my birthday!
RALEIGH. It's hard not to, May. Don't recollect the date, though.
MAY. It's next week. My birthday's next week. What is it?
RALEIGH. Open it.
MAY. The envelope or the package?
RALEIGH. Look in the envelope first. That's just to show you. Then you can keep the package.
MAY. It's a book. In the bag. I can feel it.
RALEIGH. You're a clever girl.
MAY. You're laughing at me. *(May opens the unsealed envelope and pulls out a piece of paper.)* It's a letter to you.
RALEIGH. From *The Saturday Evening Post*.
MAY. You get me a subscription?
RALEIGH. Read the letter.
MAY. "Charlie in the Back Seat." What's this about?
RALEIGH. I sold them a story. *The Saturday Evening Post* bought my story.
MAY. This story's about you and me. And Charlie.
RALEIGH. That's right.
MAY. They're gonna print a story about you and me?
RALEIGH. It's changed a little. It's a story.
MAY. That's really something. You writing for *The Saturday Evening Post*.
RALEIGH. Just like F. Scott Fitzgerald.
MAY. My word.
RALEIGH. Open the bag.

MAY. It's a book. Did you write a book?
RALEIGH. Not yet. But I've been reading this one. And I wanted you to have it.
MAY. *The Robe* by Lloyd C. Douglas. This is the new one.
RALEIGH. I hope you haven't read it.
MAY. I've been wanting to.
RALEIGH. It's real good. Slow to get into, but then it really gets interesting. Hope you don't mind that I read it first.
MAY. I don't mind. I'm glad you read it.
RALEIGH. It's a good book. Made me think a lot. It's religious.
MAY. Glad you liked it.
RALEIGH. I did. *(A pause.)*
MAY. I don't know what to say.
RALEIGH. You don't have to say anything. Just enjoy the book.
MAY. Thank you.
RALEIGH. You're welcome. *(A pause.)*
MAY. You're really leaving.
RALEIGH. Reckon I am ...
MAY. Well, you always wanted to go to New York City.
RALEIGH. Reckon I did.
MAY. And you're all better? Well enough to go?
RALEIGH. Reckon so.
MAY. You just look so good. I can't believe it.
RALEIGH. You look pretty good yourself, May.
MAY. But you've been sick.
RALEIGH. Not that sick. Might not be again. Hard to tell.
MAY. It's just inside, then. Not on the outside? Doesn't that make it worse?
RALEIGH. We're all sick on the inside, May. I think we all are.
MAY. But yours doesn't show on the outside.
RALEIGH. Eventually it all shows on the outside. Take you, for instance. Your eyes are a little duller, 'cause you've been hurt inside. And your daddy. Your daddy's gotten grayer. Your mama looks like she's been tired for a long time. Eventually it all shows on the outside. Everything we've been through.
MAY. I mean your sickness. It doesn't show on the outside yet.
RALEIGH. May, whatever are you talking about?
MAY. It doesn't show on your skin. Not where I can see, anyway.

Your skin is perfectly clear.
RALEIGH. I honestly don't have the foggiest notion of what you are referring to.
MAY. Your sickness. You said you had that disease. But it doesn't show on the outside. Is that a good thing? Will it just progress faster on the inside?
RALEIGH. Might not progress at all. Might never come back.
MAY. I didn't know that.
RALEIGH. That's what the doctor said. Might come tomorrow and might never come again.
MAY. So you did have it on your skin, then. And it healed?
RALEIGH. It's not on my skin. It's in the nerves, they think.
MAY. Then that's worse, then.
RALEIGH. Worse than what?
MAY. If it's already in the nerves it's worse than on the skin. I read about it. When I was preparing to be a missionary. It moves faster if it's inside.
RALEIGH. May, just tell me what you are talking about.
MAY. Your leprosy.
RALEIGH. My what?
MAY. Your leprosy. I've been reading all about it.
RALEIGH. You've been reading too much.
MAY. I wanted to know how to take care of you.
RALEIGH. To take care of me?
MAY. After you told me, told me at the festival, that night when you told me. The night I ran off when you got sick? After that, well, a while after, sometime after I started to write you. After you were in the hospital.
RALEIGH. May, I don't …
MAY. I thought about after you were out. You'd need someone to take care of you. To look after you when you were sick.
RALEIGH. You decided to take care — of me.
MAY. Yes.
RALEIGH. Where?
MAY. I don't know.
RALEIGH. You're gonna move to our farm? To a sharecrop?
MAY. No, well, no, that's too far out. And I have to keep my job.
RALEIGH. You're gonna care for me here at your house?

MAY. No, I thought, I thought …
RALEIGH. Just where're you going to take care of me?
MAY. Some place in town, maybe. Off Main Street.
RALEIGH. You had this all thought out, didn't you? When did you figure this all out? Didn't write it in your letters.
MAY. On my drives. To school. It's a long drive, and I'd be thinking a lot. And I sorta figured it all out. But I didn't know you were leaving.
RALEIGH. You were going to get us rooms in town.
MAY. Lots of places to rent here now.
RALEIGH. And we were just going to live there, you and me?
MAY. I'd look after you.
RALEIGH. We were going to live alone?
MAY. Well, we'd have to …
RALEIGH. We'd have to what, May?
MAY. We'd have to be …
RALEIGH. We'd have to be what, May? What would we have to be?
MAY. You know. *(A long pause.)*
RALEIGH. Are you asking me to marry you?
MAY. No.
RALEIGH. But we'd have to be married.
MAY. Yes.
RALEIGH. But you're not asking.
MAY. No.
RALEIGH. Why not?
MAY. You have to do the asking.
RALEIGH. You've got that part figured out, too.
MAY. Not really.
RALEIGH. You invited me over to dinner so I'd propose to you.
MAY. To get reacquainted.
RALEIGH. Now, let me get this straight. You are going to make a mission out of me? I am going to be your new mission. You think I need taking care of. You are going to rent a room and marry me and take care of me.
MAY. You're laughing at me.
RALEIGH. Will you marry me, May?
MAY. What?

51

RALEIGH. Will you marry me, May? Now, just how did you think this part out? Am I supposed to get down on my knees or am I on my deathbed and you are Florence Nightingale? Should I lie down so I can gaze up into those pretty eyes and ask you to marry me as I breathe my last breath? How was this scene supposed to go, May? Here, look, I'm down on my knees. I'm down on my knees and I'm proposing to you, May. Will you marry me?
MAY. You're laughing at me.
RALEIGH. Will you marry me, May?
MAY. I — are you serious? You said you were leaving town.
RALEIGH. Haven't left yet.
MAY. Are you serious?
RALEIGH. This is your story, May. Do you think I'm serious?
MAY. I don't know what to think.
RALEIGH. I wrote my story, May. Got my story published. This is your story.
MAY. You're just making fun of me.
RALEIGH. You're wrong. I'm just overwhelmed. Overwhelmed that you would ... Leprosy's contagious.
MAY. I know that.
RALEIGH. It can spread pretty fast, sometimes.
MAY. Sometimes.
RALEIGH. People care for a leper are apt to get it themselves. Even if they are careful.
MAY. I know that.
RALEIGH. We couldn't live in town long. Leprosy starts to show.
MAY. I know.
RALEIGH. They usually put lepers in a colony. A leper colony.
MAY. I've read about it.
RALEIGH. You willing to go away?
MAY. If I have to.
RALEIGH. You willing to go to a leper colony?
MAY. It might not be for a long while.
RALEIGH. You willing to go live in a leper colony? With me.
MAY. Yes, I am.
RALEIGH. You willing to leave town to take care of me.
MAY. I reckon so.
RALEIGH. To leave your family.

MAY. If I have to.
RALEIGH. That's really something. *(A pause.)* So you'd go wherever I have to go. California, Detroit, New York City.
MAY. Yes.
RALEIGH. Even go live in a leper colony.
MAY. Yes.
RALEIGH. Watching people's skin falling off. Their noses falling off. Must smell pretty bad, too. All that rotting skin. And people dying. Watching people die. You'd do that for me?
MAY. Yes. *(A pause.)*
RALEIGH. You'd go with me to a leper colony anywhere in the world, knowing that you might catch it.
MAY. Yes, I would. *(A pause.)*
RALEIGH. You're really something, May. How'd you come up with all this?
MAY. When I started writing to you. Even though you didn't write much back. I, I just figured out that you were the only one I wanted to talk to. And when you said you were leaving …
RALEIGH. You figured out you couldn't live without me.
MAY. I don't know. I reckon.
RALEIGH. Even though I have … leprosy. *(Raleigh bursts out laughing.)*
MAY. Don't laugh at me. It's not funny.
RALEIGH. You think I have leprosy?
MAY. That's what you called it.
RALEIGH. I never said I had leprosy.
MAY. At the festival. Last year at the Nibroc festival. You said the factory doctor in Detroit told you that you had leprosy.
RALEIGH. Epilepsy.
MAY. What's that?
RALEIGH. It's epilepsy, May, not leprosy. Epilepsy's the name they give to having the fits. The doctor said I have epilepsy. That's having the fits.
MAY. And that's why you were in the hospital.
RALEIGH. With the crazies. Shouldn't been in that hospital.
MAY. I thought you said leprosy.
RALEIGH. No wonder you thought I looked so good!
MAY. I thought your skin would be falling off!

RALEIGH. You sure are something, May. You sure are something.
MAY. I feel so stupid. *(A pause.)*
RALEIGH. Marry me.
MAY. You're making fun of me. You've been making fun of me.
RALEIGH. Marry me, May. Marry me now.
MAY. What do you mean?
RALEIGH. You got gasoline in the car?
MAY. Yes.
RALEIGH. Let's go right now.
MAY. To New York City?
RALEIGH. Down to Tennessee. Down to Jellico. Get married.
MAY. Right now?
RALEIGH. Right now.
MAY. I don't like to drive at night.
RALEIGH. I'll watch the road. I'll watch the road for you.
MAY. I have to teach school tomorrow. I can't miss school. I'm the principal.
RALEIGH. I'll get you back in time. Marry me tonight. Be brave.
MAY. I will. I'll marry you.
RALEIGH. Let's go. *(They start to leave but she suddenly stops.)*
MAY. Oh, Raleigh!
RALEIGH. What?
MAY. Look at it now. Look at the fire now.
RALEIGH. What about it, May?
MAY. It's burning brighter than ever.
RALEIGH. You're right. It sure is bright. Sure is burning bright.
MAY. Looks like a sunrise. *(They hold hands, staring out as the lights fade.)*

End of Play

PROPERTY LIST

Book (MAY)
Purse (MAY)
Handkerchiefs (RALEIGH, MAY)
Bank bag (MAY)
Brown paper bag containing a book (RALEIGH)
Envelope with letter (RALEIGH)
Newspaper article (RALEIGH)

SOUND EFFECTS

Train whistle
Train running on tracks
Church bells
Woods sounds
Period music, especially hymns, may be used pre-show and between scenes to mask costume and set changes.

GLOSSARY

Ashbury College: a Methodist church school in Wilmore, Kentucky.

Buggytop Shelton: a well-known bootlegger in Corbin, Kentucky, who made and sold moonshine up through the 1940s.

Dixie Dog: a restaurant on Main Street in Corbin, famous for its hot dogs with chili. As of late 1999 it was still there, still serving chili-dogs. You have to ask for ketchup.

Jake leg: a sometimes permanent paralysis caused by drinking Jamaica Gin, a tainted gin from Jamaica sold by Skinny Eaton at his pharmacy in Corbin, Kentucky, during Prohibition.

"Lamb of God": a hymn sung at revival meetings during the call to the altar, also know as "Just as I Am."

Nathanael West: author of *Day of the Locusts*, died in a car accident in California on December 22, 1940. His body was brought to New York on the Santa Fe Super Chief, which left Los Angeles at 8:00 P.M. on December 26. Also on board was Sheila Graham. Her companion, F. Scott Fitzgerald, author of *The Great Gatsby*, had died of a heart attack on December 21. Both bodies were cared for at Pierce Brothers Mortuaries, and Fitzgerald's was also sent east, to Baltimore, most likely on the same train as West.

sharecrop: a rented farm.

switch: a thin, pliable limb from a bush or small tree, used for spanking.

tent meeting: the summer revival meetings held in tents.

NEW PLAYS

★ MOTHERHOOD OUT LOUD by Leslie Ayvazian, Brooke Berman, David Cale, Jessica Goldberg, Beth Henley, Lameece Issaq, Claire LaZebnik, Lisa Loomer, Michele Lowe, Marco Pennette, Theresa Rebeck, Luanne Rice, Annie Weisman and Cheryl L. West, conceived by Susan R. Rose and Joan Stein. When entrusting the subject of motherhood to such a dazzling collection of celebrated American writers, what results is a joyous, moving, hilarious, and altogether thrilling theatrical event. "Never fails to strike both the funny bone and the heart." —*BackStage.* "Packed with wisdom, laughter, and plenty of wry surprises." —*TheaterMania.* [1M, 3W] ISBN: 978-0-8222-2589-8

★ COCK by Mike Bartlett. When John takes a break from his boyfriend, he accidentally meets the girl of his dreams. Filled with guilt and indecision, he decides there is only one way to straighten this out. "[A] brilliant and blackly hilarious feat of provocation." —*Independent.* "A smart, prickly and rewarding view of sexual and emotional confusion." —*Evening Standard.* [3M, 1W] ISBN: 978-0-8222-2766-3

★ F. Scott Fitzgerald's THE GREAT GATSBY adapted for the stage by Simon Levy. Jay Gatsby, a self-made millionaire, passionately pursues the elusive Daisy Buchanan. Nick Carraway, a young newcomer to Long Island, is drawn into their world of obsession, greed and danger. "Levy's combination of narration, dialogue and action delivers most of what is best in the novel." —*Seattle Post-Intelligencer.* "A beautifully crafted interpretation of the 1925 novel which defined the Jazz Age." —*London Free Press.* [5M, 4W] ISBN: 978-0-8222-2727-4

★ LONELY, I'M NOT by Paul Weitz. At an age when most people are discovering what they want to do with their lives, Porter has been married and divorced, earned seven figures as a corporate "ninja," and had a nervous breakdown. It's been four years since he's had a job or a date, and he's decided to give life another shot. "Critic's pick!" —*NY Times.* "An enjoyable ride." —*NY Daily News.* [3M, 3W] ISBN: 978-0-8222-2734-2

★ ASUNCION by Jesse Eisenberg. Edgar and Vinny are not racist. In fact, Edgar maintains a blog condemning American imperialism, and Vinny is three-quarters into a Ph.D. in Black Studies. When Asuncion becomes their new roommate, the boys have a perfect opportunity to demonstrate how open-minded they truly are. "Mr. Eisenberg writes lively dialogue that strikes plenty of comic sparks." —*NY Times.* "An almost ridiculously enjoyable portrait of slacker trauma among would-be intellectuals." —*Newsday.* [2M, 2W] ISBN: 978-0-8222-2630-7

DRAMATISTS PLAY SERVICE, INC.
440 Park Avenue South, New York, NY 10016 212-683-8960 Fax 212-213-1539
postmaster@dramatists.com   www.dramatists.com

NEW PLAYS

★ **THE PICTURE OF DORIAN GRAY by Roberto Aguirre-Sacasa, based on the novel by Oscar Wilde.** Preternaturally handsome Dorian Gray has his portrait painted by his college classmate Basil Hallwood. When their mutual friend Henry Wotton offers to include it in a show, Dorian makes a fateful wish—that his portrait should grow old instead of him—and strikes an unspeakable bargain with the devil. [5M, 2W] ISBN: 978-0-8222-2590-4

★ **THE LYONS by Nicky Silver.** As Ben Lyons lies dying, it becomes clear that he and his wife have been at war for many years, and his impending demise has brought no relief. When they're joined by their children all efforts at a sentimental goodbye to the dying patriarch are soon abandoned. "Hilariously frank, clear-sighted, compassionate and forgiving." –*NY Times.* "Mordant, dark and rich." –*Associated Press.* [3M, 3W] ISBN: 978-0-8222-2659-8

★ **STANDING ON CEREMONY by Mo Gaffney, Jordan Harrison, Moisés Kaufman, Neil LaBute, Wendy MacLeod, José Rivera, Paul Rudnick, and Doug Wright, conceived by Brian Shnipper.** Witty, warm and occasionally wacky, these plays are vows to the blessings of equality, the universal challenges of relationships and the often hilarious power of love. "CEREMONY puts a human face on a hot-button issue and delivers laughter and tears rather than propaganda." –*BackStage.* [3M, 3W] ISBN: 978-0-8222-2654-3

★ **ONE ARM by Moisés Kaufman, based on the short story and screenplay by Tennessee Williams.** Ollie joins the Navy and becomes the lightweight boxing champion of the Pacific Fleet. Soon after, he loses his arm in a car accident, and he turns to hustling to survive. "[A] fast, fierce, brutally beautiful stage adaptation." –*NY Magazine.* "A fascinatingly lurid, provocative and fatalistic piece of theater." –*Variety.* [7M, 1W] ISBN: 978-0-8222-2564-5

★ **AN ILIAD by Lisa Peterson and Denis O'Hare.** A modern-day retelling of Homer's classic. Poetry and humor, the ancient tale of the Trojan War and the modern world collide in this captivating theatrical experience. "Shocking, glorious, primal and deeply satisfying." –*Time Out NY.* "Explosive, altogether breathtaking." –*Chicago Sun-Times.* [1M] ISBN: 978-0-8222-2687-1

★ **THE COLUMNIST by David Auburn.** At the height of the Cold War, Joe Alsop is the nation's most influential journalist, beloved, feared and courted by the Washington world. But as the '60s dawn and America undergoes dizzying change, the intense political dramas Joe is embroiled in become deeply personal as well. "Intensely satisfying." –*Bloomberg News.* [5M, 2W] ISBN: 978-0-8222-2699-4

DRAMATISTS PLAY SERVICE, INC.
440 Park Avenue South, New York, NY 10016   212-683-8960   Fax 212-213-1539
postmaster@dramatists.com   www.dramatists.com

NEW PLAYS

★ **BENGAL TIGER AT THE BAGHDAD ZOO by Rajiv Joseph.** The lives of two American Marines and an Iraqi translator are forever changed by an encounter with a quick-witted tiger who haunts the streets of war-torn Baghdad. "[A] boldly imagined, harrowing and surprisingly funny drama." *–NY Times.* "Tragic yet darkly comic and highly imaginative." *–CurtainUp.* [5M, 2W] ISBN: 978-0-8222-2565-2

★ **THE PITMEN PAINTERS by Lee Hall, inspired by a book by William Feaver.** Based on the triumphant true story, a group of British miners discover a new way to express themselves and unexpectedly become art-world sensations. "Excitingly ambiguous, in-the-moment theater." *–NY Times.* "Heartfelt, moving and deeply politicized." *–Chicago Tribune.* [5M, 2W] ISBN: 978-0-8222-2507-2

★ **RELATIVELY SPEAKING by Ethan Coen, Elaine May and Woody Allen.** In TALKING CURE, Ethan Coen uncovers the sort of insanity that can only come from family. Elaine May explores the hilarity of passing in GEORGE IS DEAD. In HONEYMOON MOTEL, Woody Allen invites you to the sort of wedding day you won't forget. "Firecracker funny." *–NY Times.* "A rollicking good time." *–New Yorker.* [8M, 7W] ISBN: 978-0-8222-2394-8

★ **SONS OF THE PROPHET by Stephen Karam.** If to live is to suffer, then Joseph Douaihy is more alive than most. With unexplained chronic pain and the fate of his reeling family on his shoulders, Joseph's health, sanity, and insurance premium are on the line. "Explosively funny." *–NY Times.* "At once deep, deft and beautifully made." *–New Yorker.* [5M, 3W] ISBN: 978-0-8222-2597-3

★ **THE MOUNTAINTOP by Katori Hall.** A gripping reimagination of events the night before the assassination of the civil rights leader Dr. Martin Luther King, Jr. "An ominous electricity crackles through the opening moments." *–NY Times.* "[A] thrilling, wild, provocative flight of magical realism." *–Associated Press.* "Crackles with theatricality and a humanity more moving than sainthood." *–NY Newsday.* [1M, 1W] ISBN: 978-0-8222-2603-1

★ **ALL NEW PEOPLE by Zach Braff.** Charlie is 35, heartbroken, and just wants some time away from the rest of the world. Long Beach Island seems to be the perfect escape until his solitude is interrupted by a motley parade of misfits who show up and change his plans. "Consistently and sometimes sensationally funny." *–NY Times.* "A morbidly funny play about the trendy new existential condition of being young, adorable, and miserable." *–Variety.* [2M, 2W] ISBN: 978-0-8222-2562-1

DRAMATISTS PLAY SERVICE, INC.
440 Park Avenue South, New York, NY 10016   212-683-8960   Fax 212-213-1539
postmaster@dramatists.com   www.dramatists.com

NEW PLAYS

★ **CLYBOURNE PARK by Bruce Norris.** WINNER OF THE 2011 PULITZER PRIZE AND 2012 TONY AWARD. Act One takes place in 1959 as community leaders try to stop the sale of a home to a black family. Act Two is set in the same house in the present day as the now predominantly African-American neighborhood battles to hold its ground. "Vital, sharp-witted and ferociously smart." –*NY Times*. "A theatrical treasure…Indisputably, uproariously funny." –*Entertainment Weekly*. [4M, 3W] ISBN: 978-0-8222-2697-0

★ **WATER BY THE SPOONFUL by Quiara Alegría Hudes.** WINNER OF THE 2012 PULITZER PRIZE. A Puerto Rican veteran is surrounded by the North Philadelphia demons he tried to escape in the service. "This is a very funny, warm, and yes uplifting play." –*Hartford Courant*. "The play is a combination poem, prayer and app on how to cope in an age of uncertainty, speed and chaos." –*Variety*. [4M, 3W] ISBN: 978-0-8222-2716-8

★ **RED by John Logan.** WINNER OF THE 2010 TONY AWARD. Mark Rothko has just landed the biggest commission in the history of modern art. But when his young assistant, Ken, gains the confidence to challenge him, Rothko faces the agonizing possibility that his crowning achievement could also become his undoing. "Intense and exciting." –*NY Times*. "Smart, eloquent entertainment." –*New Yorker*. [2M] ISBN: 978-0-8222-2483-9

★ **VENUS IN FUR by David Ives.** Thomas, a beleaguered playwright/director, is desperate to find an actress to play Vanda, the female lead in his adaptation of the classic sadomasochistic tale *Venus in Fur*. "Ninety minutes of good, kinky fun." –*NY Times*. "A fast-paced journey into one man's entrapment by a clever, vengeful female." –*Associated Press*. [1M, 1W] ISBN: 978-0-8222-2603-1

★ **OTHER DESERT CITIES by Jon Robin Baitz.** Brooke returns home to Palm Springs after a six-year absence and announces that she is about to publish a memoir dredging up a pivotal and tragic event in the family's history—a wound they don't want reopened. "Leaves you feeling both moved and gratifyingly sated." –*NY Times*. "A genuine pleasure." –*NY Post*. [2M, 3W] ISBN: 978-0-8222-2605-5

★ **TRIBES by Nina Raine.** Billy was born deaf into a hearing family and adapts brilliantly to his family's unconventional ways, but it's not until he meets Sylvia, a young woman on the brink of deafness, that he finally understands what it means to be understood. "A smart, lively play." –*NY Times*. "[A] bright and boldly provocative drama." –*Associated Press*. [3M, 2W] ISBN: 978-0-8222-2751-9

DRAMATISTS PLAY SERVICE, INC.
440 Park Avenue South, New York, NY 10016 212-683-8960 Fax 212-213-1539
postmaster@dramatists.com   www.dramatists.com